Platypus

Sara Antill

WINDMILL BOOKS

New York

Published in 2011 by Windmill Books, LLC
303 Park Avenue South, Suite # 1280, New York, NY 10010-3657

First Edition

CREDITS:
Author: Sara Antill
Edited by: Jennifer Way
Designed by: Brian Garvey

Photo Credits: Cover, p. 4–5 Theo Allofs/Getty Images; cover background, pp. 5 (bottom left, bottom right), 7 (top, bottom), 9, 11, 21 Shutterstock.com; p. 5 (top) © www.iStockphoto.com/Samuel Kessler; pp. 6–7 © Juniors Bildarchiv/age fotostock; p. 8 © Biosphoto/Watts Dave/Peter Arnold Inc.; pp. 10 (inset), 14–15, 18–19, 22 (bottom) Jason Edwards/Getty Images; p. 10 © www.iStockphoto.com/Wouter Tolenaars; pp. 12–13, 22 (top) © J Hauke/age fotostock; p. 14 (inset) © www.iStockphoto.com/George Clerk; p. 16 (inset) © www.iStockphoto.com/tomograf; p. 16–17 © Dave Watts/age fotostock; p. 20 © Roland Seitre/Peter Arnold Inc.

Library of Congress Cataloging-in-Publication Data

Antill, Sara.
  Platypus / by Sara Antill. — 1st ed.
      p. cm. — (Unusual animals)
  Includes index.
  ISBN 978-1-60754-991-8 (library binding) — ISBN 978-1-60754-997-0 (pbk.) —
  ISBN 978-1-60754-998-7 (6-pack)
  1. Platypus—Juvenile literature. I. Title.
  QL737.M72A68 2011
  599.2'9—dc22
                      2010004431

Manufactured in the United States of America

For more great fiction and nonfiction, go to windmillbooks.com.

CPSIA Compliance Information: Batch # BW2011WM: For Further Information contact Windmill Books, New York, New York at 1-866-478-0556

Table of Contents

A Strange Creature

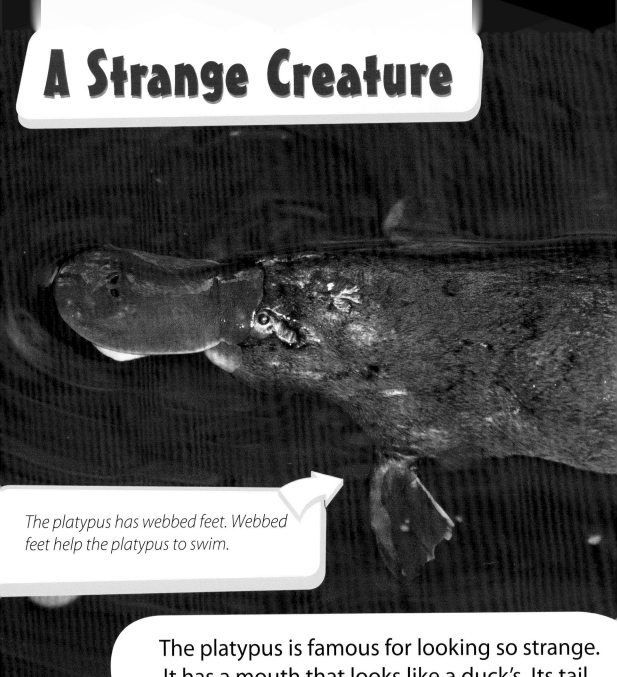

The platypus has webbed feet. Webbed feet help the platypus to swim.

The platypus is famous for looking so strange. It has a mouth that looks like a duck's. Its tail looks like a beaver's. And its body looks like an otter's!

The platypus is an animal that lives in eastern Australia and Tasmania. When an **explorer** in Australia sent the first platypus to Europe, many people thought that it was a **hoax**. No one had seen anything like a platypus before!

Duck

Otter

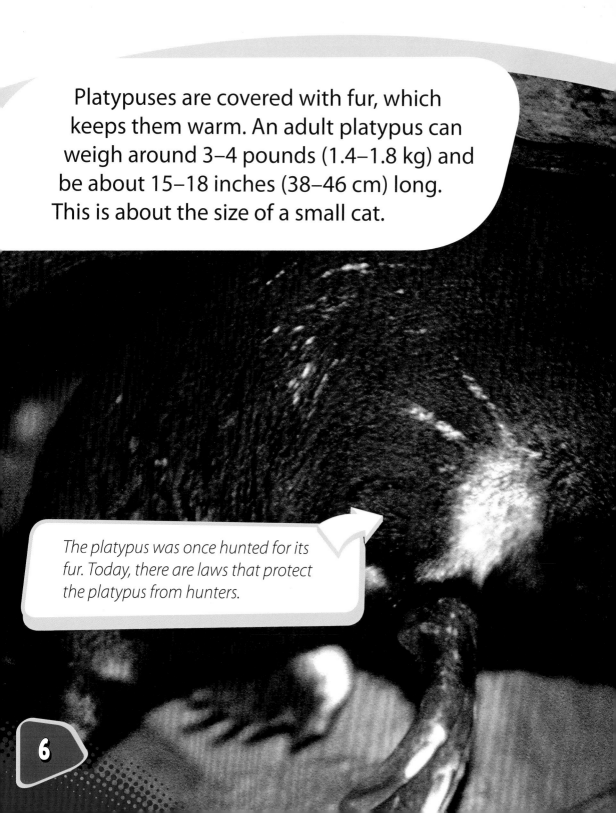

Platypuses are covered with fur, which keeps them warm. An adult platypus can weigh around 3–4 pounds (1.4–1.8 kg) and be about 15–18 inches (38–46 cm) long. This is about the size of a small cat.

The platypus was once hunted for its fur. Today, there are laws that protect the platypus from hunters.

Platypuses can live for 12 to 15 years. Their biggest threats in the wild are snakes, foxes, rats, and **pollution** from humans.

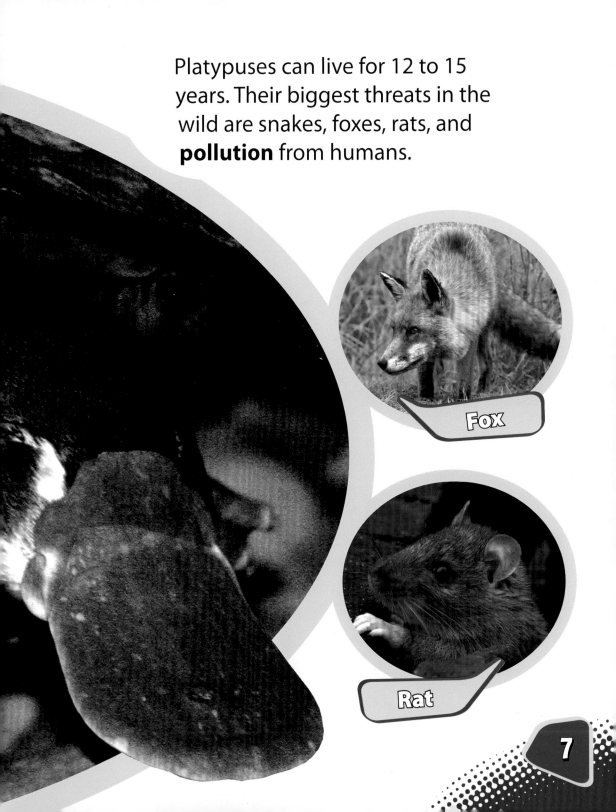

Fox

Rat

A Double Life

The platypus is **semiaquatic**. That means it spends some of its time on land, and some of it in the water.

This platypus is resting in its burrow. The burrow is built next to a river.

Platypuses dig their **burrows** near rivers and streams. Burrows are holes in the ground where platypuses live. They use their nails and feet to dig these holes.

Platypuses swim in freshwater rivers and streams like the one shown here.

Platypuses have a thin piece of skin between their toes. Its webbed feet make the platypus a very good swimmer.

Platypus Foot

The platypus's legs work like paddles in the water. This helps it to swim.

In the water, platypuses use their front two webbed feet to paddle. They use their back two webbed feet and tail to **steer** themselves in the right direction.

Platypuses hunt for their food in the water. Pieces of skin over their eyes and ears help to keep the water out. A platypus can stay underwater for more than two minutes!

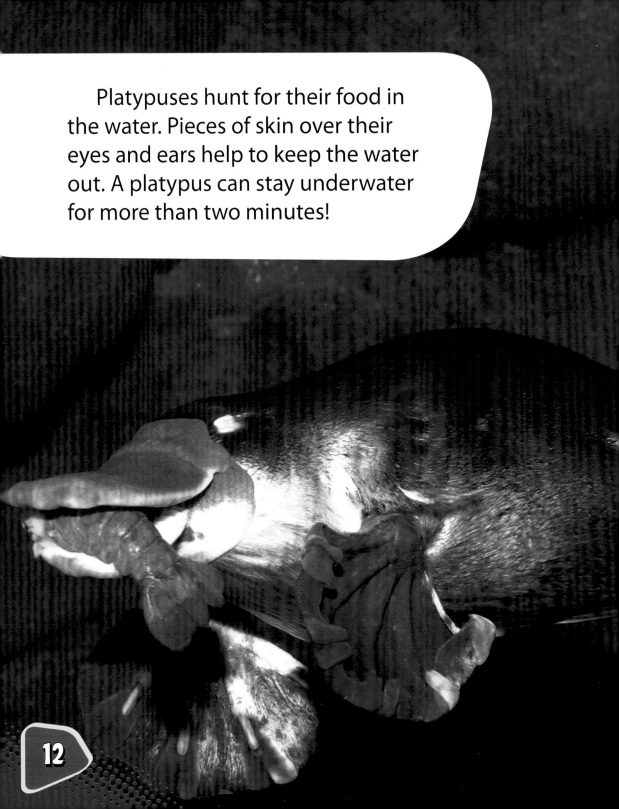

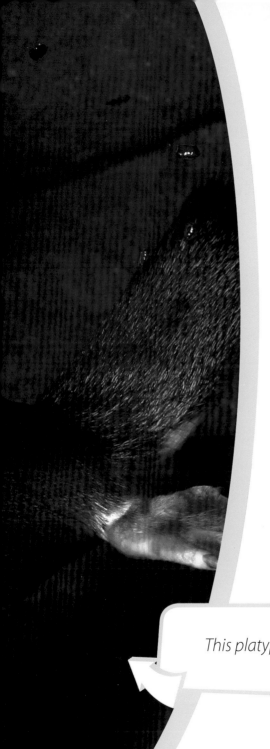

Platypuses eat mostly worms, shellfish, and insects. They don't have teeth, so small rocks and sand in their mouths help them "chew" their food.

This platypus is eating a freshwater crayfish.

Male platypuses have a hollow spine on the back of each hind leg. These two sharp spines release a dangerous **venom**.

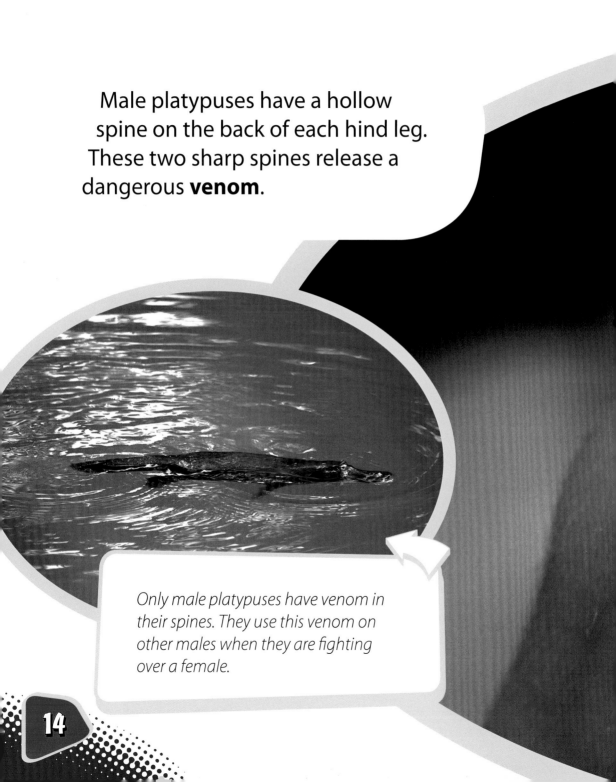

Only male platypuses have venom in their spines. They use this venom on other males when they are fighting over a female.

An Egg-Laying Mammal?

The platypus is a **mammal**. Mammals are warm-blooded animals that feed their babies with milk. Mammals usually give birth to live babies, instead of laying eggs.

AUSTRALIA 36ᶜ

Year

PLATYPUS

Australian postage stamp

The platypus may look strange, but it is different from other mammals in another big way. The platypus is one of only two mammals to lay eggs instead of giving birth to live young.

The platypus is unlike any other animal in the world. This makes many people in Australia very proud. Platypuses are pictured on Australia's coins and stamps.

These baby platypuses were born at a zoo in Australia.

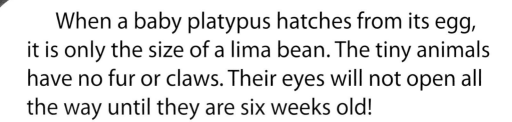

When a baby platypus hatches from its egg, it is only the size of a lima bean. The tiny animals have no fur or claws. Their eyes will not open all the way until they are six weeks old!

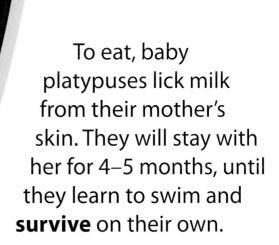

To eat, baby platypuses lick milk from their mother's skin. They will stay with her for 4–5 months, until they learn to swim and **survive** on their own.

For a long time, people hunted platypuses for their fur. Today, there are laws that protect the platypus from hunters. But platypuses still get trapped in fishing nets and drown.

Scientists put a small computer chip under this platypus's skin. This helps them find the platypus in the wild.

Dirty, polluted rivers like this are unsafe for a playtypus.

Platypuses are also in danger from **litter** and water pollution. Dirty rivers and streams make life unhealthy for the platypus, and for the animals that it eats. For the platypus, a clean, healthy river is a clean, healthy home!

Inside Story

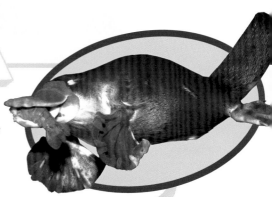

A platypus needs to eat for 12 hours each day just to stay alive!

The growl of a platypus sounds a lot like the growl of a puppy.

A baby platypus is born with teeth, but they fall out before they are ever used!

Glossary

BURROW (BUR-oh) A hole in the ground that an animal digs to live or hide in.

EXPLORER (ek-SPLOR-er) Someone who travels to a new place that not many other people have seen, to discover new things about that place.

HOAX (hohks) A trick.

LITTER (LIH-dur) Any kind of garbage or waste that is thrown into nature.

MAMMAL (MA-mull) A warm-blooded animal that usually gives birth to live young instead of laying eggs.

POLLUTION (puh-LOO-shun) Waste that is released into nature and makes an environment dirty and unhealthy.

SEMIAQUATIC (she-mee-uh-KWAH-tik) Living part of the time on the land and part of the time in the water.

STEER (STEER) To make something move in a certain direction.

SURVIVE (sur-VYV) To stay alive.

VENOM (VEH-num) A poison that some animals can release by biting or stinging.

Index

Read More

Arnold, Caroline. *A Platypus' World*. Mankato, MN: Picture Window Books, 2008.

Caper, William. *Platypus: A Century-long Mystery*. New York: Bearport Publishing, 2008.

Clarke, Ginjer L. *Platypus!*. New York: Random House, 2004.

Web Sites

For Web resources related to the subject of this book, go to: **www.windmillbooks.com/weblinks** and select this book's title.